TURNING POINTS
IN HISTORY

Revised and Updated

D1809911

Heinemann
LIBRARY

The Fall of the
Berlin Wall

old War Ends

www.heinemann.co.uk
Visit our website to find out more information about **Heinemann Library** books.

To order:
 Phone 44 (0) 1865 888112
 Send a fax to 44 (0) 1865 314091
Visit the Heinemann Bookshop at www.heinemann.co.uk/library to browse our catalogue and order online.

First published in Great Britain by
Heinemann Library,
Halley Court, Jordan Hill, Oxford OX2 8EJ,
part of Harcourt Education.
Heinemann is a registered trademark of
Harcourt Education Ltd.

Editorial: Clare Lewis
Designed by Tokay Interactive Ltd.
(www.tokay.co.uk)
Map artwork by Robert Sydenham,
Ambassador Design Ltd
Printed in China by WKT Company Limited

13 digit ISBN: 978 0 431 07705 5 (hb)
10 09 08 07 06
10 9 8 7 6 5 4 3 2 1

13 digit ISBN: 978 0 431 07769 7 (pb)
12 11 10 09 08
10 9 8 7 6 5 4 3 2 1

**British Library Cataloguing in
Publication Data**
Kelly, Nigel
Turning Points in History: The Fall of the
Berlin Wall: the Cold War ends – 2nd edition
943.1'55'087
A full catalogue record for this book is
available from the British Library.

Acknowledgements
The Publishers would like to thank the
following for permission to reproduce
photographs:
Bridgeman: p. **6**; Centre for the Study of
Cartoon and Caricature: pp. **10**, **18**; Corbis:
(AFP) p. **4**, (Bettman) pp. **16**, **17**, pp. **23**,
25; Hulton Getty: pp. **8**, **15**; King, David:
pp. **7**, **11**; Magnum Photos: (Joseph
Koudelka) p. **21**; Rex Features: p. **20**;
hone/Gamma/Frank Spooner pictures:
p. **28**; Sipa Press: p. **24**.

Cover photograph reproduced with
permission of Empics/AP Photo/John Gaps III.

The publishers would like to thank Stewart
Ross for his help in the preparation of this
book.

Every effort has been made to contact
copyright holders of any material reproduced
in this book. Any omissions will be rectified
in subsequent printings if notice is given to
the Publisher.

Contents

Some words are shown in bold, **like this**. You can find out what they mean by looking in the Glossary.

The wall comes down

Knocking down the wall

On 9 November 1989 people all over Germany celebrated the decision to knock down a wall. However, it was not just any wall – it was the most hated boundary in history. This concrete barrier, 5 metres (16 feet) high, was a symbol of the division between two different political beliefs and two different ways of life. The **Berlin Wall** did not just divide East and West Berlin, it was also the division between the **communists** of Eastern Europe and the **democracies** of Western Europe and the United States – known as the West.

The people of Berlin hated the wall because its creation had split families and friends and divided their city in two. But what made the people so happy that night in 1989 was that they saw the breaching of the wall as a sign of a much more important event in international relations. For more than 40 years the countries of Eastern Europe and those of the West, led by the United States, had been involved in a **Cold War**.

Tearing down the hated Berlin Wall – just a few days before this, anyone attacking the wall would have been shot dead!

The Cold War

The Cold War was not a military war. Instead it was a war of words where the two sides, East and West, tried to extend their influence and score victories. They used **propaganda** to emphasize their own good points or discredit their opponents. Many people feared that the world was constantly on the brink of a real war.

During the Cold War, both East and West poured a lot of money into researching and developing more and more advanced weapons.

CAPITALISM   COMMUNISM

Wealthy people (**capitalists**) invest their money in land and industry. Their companies employ workers and keep the profits that are made. A capitalist system usually has a democratic government, with a number of political parties.

There is a classless society. There is no individual profit-making, and land and industry are owned by the state. Profits are used for the good of all. There is only one political party.

| Communism and capitalism

Each side wanted to have greater military power than the other. Among their weapons were atomic bombs, which had first been used by the Americans on Hiroshima in 1945 at the end of World War II. Such weapons led to a fear that the Cold War might turn "hot", resulting in widescale destruction and millions of deaths.

What the people of Berlin were hoping was that if the very symbol of this Cold War – the Berlin Wall – came down, then surely the Cold War itself would soon end. East and West might be able to live in peace and co-operate. If this proved to be the case, the fall of the Berlin Wall would truly be a turning point in world history.

Into a new world

"Even though it is the middle of the night, we woke up the children and brought them to the wall for this historic occasion. It is important that they see the tremendous things that are happening here…"

These were the words of a 41-year-old man living in East Berlin on 9 November 1989. As he spoke, hundreds of young East and West Berliners were climbing to the top of the wall to greet each other. Many of them used chisels and hammers to chip away souvenirs of the historic night.

How it all began

The Russian Revolution

The seeds of the Cold War date back to 1917. In that year the last **tsar** of Russia was overthrown and eventually replaced by a **Bolshevik** (later renamed communist) government. The name of the country – Russia – was changed to the **Soviet Union**.

The governments of the West did not approve of the new communist system and they wanted to destroy it. They sent troops to Russia to help forces fighting against the communists in a bitter **civil war**. The communists won and became the undisputed rulers of Russia. However, the communist leaders did not trust the West and were convinced that if any chance arose to destroy communism, the West would take it.

Distrust

In the West the capitalist countries were just as suspicious. They thought that the Soviet Union wanted to spread communism worldwide by overthrowing the existing governments of other countries and replacing them with communist ones. The Western countries were just as distrustful of the Soviet Union as it was of them.

In November 1917, Bolshevik troops stormed the Winter Palace, which was the headquarters of the Russian regional government, and seized power.

Adolf Hitler

In the 1930s there was a chance for the two sides to put their differences aside and become friends. They were both very concerned when, in 1933, Adolf Hitler became the new German leader. He promised the German people he would make their country strong again and win back what it had lost in World War I (1914–18).

A Soviet cartoon from the 1930s. It is criticizing Britain and France, whose leaders are shown directing Hitler and his generals away from the West and towards the Soviet Union. The Soviets thought that Britain and France were being friendly to Hitler so that he would destroy the Soviet Union.

The Soviet Union was worried because Hitler hated communism and wanted to gain Soviet lands. The West was also worried. The United States was trying not to be drawn into other countries' affairs. Both Britain and France knew that if Germany became strong again, it might want to fight another war. To try to avoid this they had a policy of **appeasement** towards Germany. This meant that they gave in to Hitler's demands as long as they did not seem too unreasonable. They were determined not to see the casualties of World War I repeated. The Soviets thought that the West was being friendly with Hitler in the hope that he would attack the Soviet Union. If he did, Germany and the Soviet Union would both become weaker, which would suit the West.

The best thing would have been for the West and the Soviet Union to join together as **allies** after 1933, but they distrusted each other too much for that. In the end there was an astonishing agreement in 1939 between the Soviet Union and Germany, called the Nazi–Soviet Pact. The two countries hated each other, but for the moment it suited them to be allies.

Deteriorating relations

Despite the policy of appeasement, World War II broke out in Europe in September 1939. Within two years the Soviet Union and Germany were at war.

Now that they were all fighting **Nazi** Germany, Britain, the United States, France, and the Soviet Union became allies. However, even when they were fighting on the same side, the West and the Soviet Union were still suspicious of each other. The Western countries were determined to make sure that the Soviet Union did not become even more powerful after the war. This was to prove very difficult.

The Germans had invaded the Soviet Union in 1941, but by 1945 they had been defeated. Advancing from the east and west, the troops of the Soviet Union and its allies moved slowly across Europe and into Germany. Eventually the Soviets captured Berlin, Germany surrendered, and the war in Europe was over.

The Soviet empire

As the Soviet Army advanced across Europe, it liberated (freed) many countries from Nazi rule. These countries, which included Hungary and Czechoslovakia, were grateful to the Soviet Union and many of their people were happy to elect communists to govern them. However, sometimes the Soviet leader, Josef Stalin, used force to make sure that countries co-operated with the communists. Soon communist governments loyal to the Soviet Union had been set up across Eastern Europe. The Soviet Union had also moved its own border 480 kilometres (300 miles) west by taking over territory in Latvia, Lithuania, Estonia, and Poland.

Soviet troops and American troops meet in Berlin in April 1945. For the moment they were great friends, but the friendship was not to last.

The fears of the West

The Soviet Union thought that it was protecting itself by setting up friendly communist governments in Eastern Europe. The Western countries, however – particularly the United States – saw what Stalin was doing as the first step towards spreading communism through Europe and across the world.

Winston Churchill, who had been prime minister of Britain during the war, spoke of how an "**Iron Curtain**" had been drawn across Europe by Stalin. This name soon stuck, as a 1,600-kilometre (1,000-mile) series of fences – protected by razor wire, dog runs, guard towers, and remote-control weapons – was erected to separate East and West Europe.

The United States decided to take steps to stop this "communist advance". In March 1947 US President Harry S. Truman said that his country would help any government threatened either from within or from outside its own borders. This was the **Truman Doctrine**. In June 1947 Truman announced the **Marshall Plan**. In this, the United States offered huge grants to help European countries recover from the war. Stalin banned the countries of Eastern Europe from applying for these grants. The friendly relations that had grown during World War II were soon gone.

The map legend:
- Territory gained by USSR in 1945
- Countries under communist control
- Communist but independent
- Iron Curtain

The Iron Curtain – how Europe was divided after World War II

The Iron Curtain

"From Stettin in the Baltic to Trieste in the Adriatic, an Iron Curtain has descended across the continent … the growth of communist parties in these countries poses a growing challenge to Christian civilization."

Winston Churchill speaking to a US audience in March 1946. He was very suspicious of Soviet actions, but since the war had only just finished, not everyone shared his anxieties. Some Americans felt that Churchill was being too tough on the Soviet Union.

Communism v capitalism

Superpower rivalry

The distrust that the East and West had for each other, and the division of Europe by the Iron Curtain, resulted in almost 40 years of bitter rivalry in what became known as the Cold War. The leading players in this rivalry were the United States and the Soviet Union. These two countries were so large and powerful that historians often refer to them as **superpowers**.

The Soviet Union dominated Eastern Europe and made sure that the communist governments in countries behind the Iron Curtain were loyal to its leadership. The United States did not control Western Europe in the same way, but as the world's richest country, it had great influence and was generally accepted as the leader of the West by countries such as France and Britain.

Containing communism

During this period, one of the major aims of the United States was to prevent the further spread of communism. The Americans called this a policy of "containment" and the Marshall Plan was part of this policy. The Americans believed that when people were unhappy, beliefs such as communism were likely to sound very attractive. Unhappiness is often caused by poverty. There was plenty of poverty in Europe after the war. Between 1948 and 1952 the Americans provided $13 billion to help European countries fight poverty and recover from problems created by the war.

"Come on, Sam! It's up to us again"

An American cartoon showing "Uncle Sam", (representing the United States), being asked to help Western Europe. It is clearly in his interests to do so!

This propoganda painting shows the Soviet leader, Josef Stalin, meeting industrial workers. From the picture, they all look very happy, but the true situation was very different.

Different views

It is interesting to note that in 1947, a leading Soviet official described the Marshall Plan as "an American plan to enslave Europe". It is clear that the two sides saw things differently and there was much distrust and misunderstanding during the Cold War.

Of course, the Soviet Union was also issuing propaganda. One effective way it did this was by showing how popular communism was in the Soviet Union. The painting above gives a very positive impression of workers' relationship with their leader, Stalin. Who would guess from this that workers complained bitterly about long hours and low pay in the Soviet Union or that Stalin sent an estimated 20 million people to **labour camps**, where over half of them died?

The Marshall Plan – opposing views

The cartoon opposite shows how the Americans saw the Marshall Plan. It suggests that Uncle Sam (who represents the United States) is going to have to rescue Western Europe again. The cartoon is a piece of propaganda. That means that it is exaggerating the truth to get a point across.

Notice how the Americans' garden looks very neat and how, without US help, Western Europe's house is going to fall down. The message of the cartoon is that the United States is a kind and helpful country that runs its affairs well and will help Europe. The cartoon also has a message for the US people. If the European house falls down it will fall on the American house. The cartoonist clearly thinks that if Western Europe became communist, the United States would be under threat too.

The Berlin blockade

After World War II Berlin was divided into four zones, each governed by one of the four allies in the war (Britain, the United States, France, and the Soviet Union). By 1948 Britain, France, and the United States had decided to join their areas together and introduce a new currency to try to make the unified area more prosperous. Stalin was worried because this would make the Soviet zone look poor in comparison. He did not have the money to build it up to the same level as the Western zones. He objected to the other three allies having any control of Berlin because the city was in the part of Germany controlled by the Soviet Union.

On 24 June 1948 Stalin decided to try to force the three Western countries to give up their zones. He set up a **blockade** by cutting all road, rail, and canal links between the British, French, and American parts of Germany and their zones in Berlin (now called West Berlin). He knew that West Berlin had enough food and fuel for only six weeks and he expected the three Western allies to let the Soviet Union have its way. As far as he could see, their only alternative was to use tanks to smash through the road and rail blocks and bring in supplies. Such an aggressive action was bound to cause war and he doubted whether they would do that.

The division of Germany and Berlin after World War II. Each of the four victorious forces (the United States, Britain, France, and the Soviet Union) took control of an area of Berlin.

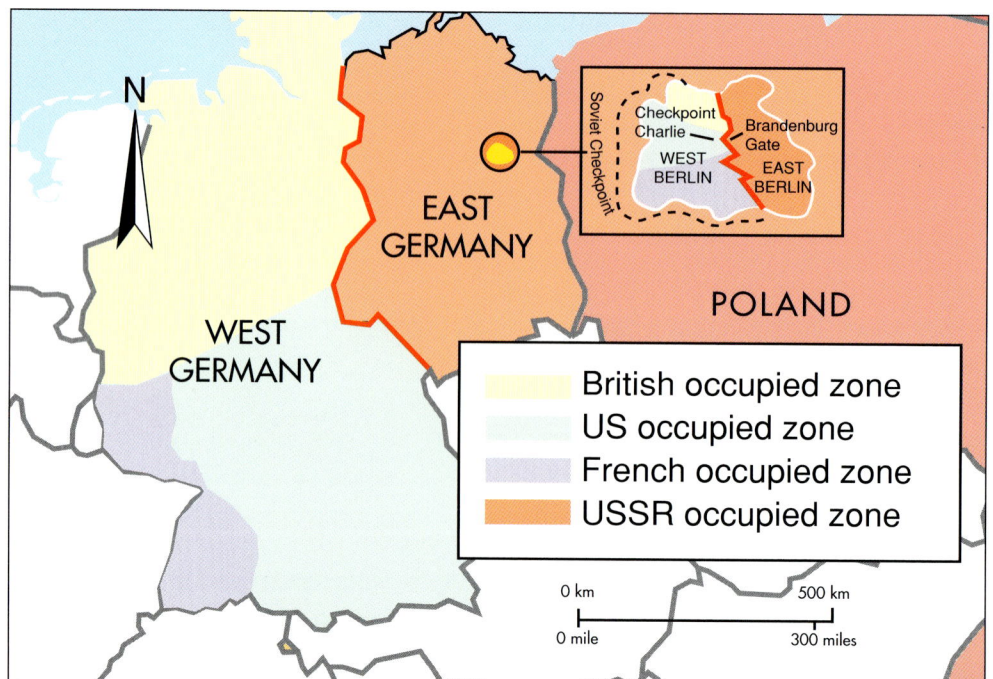

President Clinton

In 1998 US President Bill Clinton visited Berlin to celebrate the 50th anniversary of the Berlin blockade and airlift. In his speech he called Berlin "the first battlefield of the Cold War". No one really thought that it was possible to supply a city from the air, but a few forward-thinking people were convinced it could be done.

The Berlin airlift

Stalin had not counted on the West's determination to keep West Berlin. The West decided to fly supplies into the city. If Stalin wanted to stop the supplies, he would have to shoot the planes down. What would people think of a leader who shot down planes carrying food and fuel to people in need? To help persuade Stalin that shooting down the planes would be an unwise move, the Americans stationed B-29 bombers in Britain – ready to drop atomic bombs on the Soviet Union if necessary.

This postcard was sent by a grateful child in West Berlin. The message reads "130 days airlift. We thank the pilots for your work and effort".

Over the next 11 months the three Western allies made 275,000 air trips from their bases in Germany into West Berlin. They delivered over 2 million tonnes of supplies. Eventually Stalin had to accept that the West was committed to keeping West Berlin – and he called off his blockade.

Little "vittles" – candy parachutes

During the airlift an American pilot called Gail S. Halvorsen began making small parachutes out of scraps of cloth. He used them to drop candy (sweets) to children in West Berlin. As news of his action spread, donations of thousands of dollars worth of sweets and scrap cloth came in from across the United States. By January 1949 more than 250,000 "candy parachutes" had been dropped to the excited and grateful children of West Berlin.

13

Building the wall

Stalin had hoped that people living in East Berlin and the Soviet-controlled zone of Germany (from 1949 it was called East Germany) would not feel that West Berlin was a more attractive place to live. The capitalist system and money from the Western allies made West Germany more prosperous, with higher wages and a higher standard of living. From May 1949 to 1961 an estimated 2.5 million people left East Germany to live and work in the West. Many of them were skilled engineers and professional people whose talents were much needed in the East. In 1960, for example, 688 doctors, 296 dentists, and 2,648 engineers crossed over.

Stopping the flow

In June 1961 the Soviet leader, Nikita Khrushchev, demanded that the Western powers leave Berlin. The US President John F. Kennedy flew to West Berlin to assure the people living there that he would not allow them to fall under communist control. The people were delighted to hear him say, "Ich bin ein Berliner" (I am a Berliner) – though in German a *Berliner* is actually a doughnut!

Khrushchev decided that if the Western allies would not leave West Berlin, he would cut all contact between the two halves of the city. It was already virtually impossible for people "behind the Iron Curtain" to cross to the West – except from East Berlin to West Berlin.

The number of East Germans crossing into West Germany during the period of 1949–62. Notice the dramatic drop in numbers after the Wall was built in 1961.

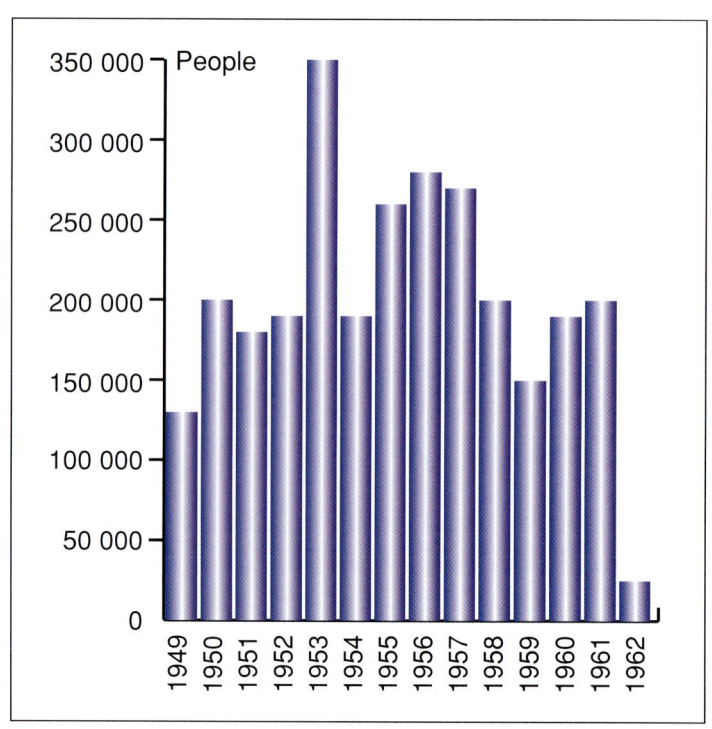

The Berlin Wall, dividing East and West Berlin

Plugging the gap

Now it was time to mend "the hole" in the Iron Curtain, through which so many of East Germany's skilled people were leaving.

On 13 August 1961 the East German government erected a border of machine guns and barbed wire between East and West Berlin. Three days later work started on a 45-kilometre (30-mile) concrete wall. It was announced that anyone trying to cross the wall would be shot.

The memories of Margit Hosseini

Margit Hosseini lived in West Berlin when the wall was built. In 1996 she gave an interview that provided many useful insights into what life was like in the city.

Life before the wall was built: "The main difference between East Berlin and West Berlin showed in clothes. If we ever visited East Berlin we always took clothes because ours were much nicer. We also took oranges, because oranges were unobtainable in East Berlin."

An incident at the wall: "I was staying with friends near the wall and we heard something was happening. We went to look. There was a wounded man lying in the border zone. At first he screamed, he cried, he shouted for help. And as the hours went on, his voice got weaker, until he stopped. I felt it was so heart-rending that in the middle of nowhere was a human being dying and the two groups were facing each other too worried to act. I was just crying — it was really horrible. I am sure the soldiers felt the same, on both sides."

This incident was probably the failed attempt to cross the wall, described on page 17.

Crossing the wall

At first there were some problems for the East German authorities trying to stop people crossing the Berlin Wall. In places the wall ran past buildings that became part of the dividing line between East and West Berlin. In the first few weeks after the building of the wall, some East Germans leapt from windows in these buildings to be caught by the crowd below. One 59-year-old woman threw a mattress out of an upper-floor window and jumped into West Berlin. She died of her injuries.

The West Berlin fire department began sending firemen with blankets to catch people jumping from upper-floor windows. In one famous case a woman tried to jump out of a window and was held back by East German police as West German firemen waited below to catch her. She eventually managed to break free and was caught safely by the firemen.

A German woman being lowered from East Berlin to West

Failed attempts

Although there were many spectacular escapes, the windows of buildings on the border were soon bricked up and machine-gun posts, minefields, and guards prevented safe crossing. Forty-one East Germans lost their lives crossing the wall in its first year. Amongst them was a young man called Peter Fechter.

The body of Peter Fechter lies in Soviet-controlled territory, close to the Berlin Wall. He almost made it to the West.

Peter Fechter

Peter Fechter was an 18-year-old bricklayer from East Berlin. In 1962 he decided to cross the Berlin Wall to be with his sister, Hilfe, in West Berlin. Together with a friend, he dashed across a border of sand and began scaling the wall. His friend managed to get over the barbed wire on top of the wall, but Fechter hesitated and was shot in the back by the border police. He fell back to the ground and lay bleeding to death. He could be heard crying pitifully for help.

Just 300 metres (980 feet) away was a US command post, Checkpoint Charlie. Crowds on the West Berlin side begged the Americans to rescue the boy but the soldiers on patrol were ordered not to intervene. Fechter was in Soviet-controlled territory and any intervention might cause an international incident. Fifty-five minutes after he had been shot his body was taken away by East Berlin guards. He was the 50th East German to die trying to cross the wall.

The Cuban missile crisis

Part of the Cold War was a deadly contest to have more and better weapons than the other side. By 1962 the Soviet Union and the United States had built up huge stockpiles of nuclear weapons and could even fire missiles from nuclear submarines under the sea. Each of the superpowers had nuclear missile bases, although the United States had the advantage of being more or less out of range of Soviet missiles.

A cartoon from a British newspaper showing Kennedy, Khrushchev, and Castro as gunslingers from the old American West. The cartoonist is suggesting that the Cuban missile crisis was really a personal contest of strength between them.

On the brink of war

Cuba is an island just 150 kilometres (93 miles) off the coast of the United States. From 1959 its leader was Fidel Castro, who was friendly with the Soviet Union. In April 1961 US President Kennedy supported an attempt to overthrow Castro, but it was defeated and the Americans were made to look foolish. Castro was angered and became even friendlier with the Soviet Union.

The missile threat

In October 1962 American spy planes found evidence of sites for nuclear missiles on Cuba. News also reached Kennedy that a Soviet fleet was heading for Cuba, carrying what looked like missiles. If missile bases were successfully established on Cuba, virtually the whole of the United States would be threatened. Kennedy would not allow this to happen.

Crisis time

Kennedy decided to put a blockade around Cuba and not let any ships through. He also called on Khrushchev to remove the missiles already in Cuba. Khrushchev refused. He said the West had nuclear weapons stationed in countries all around the Soviet Union, such as Turkey and Iran, and so had no right to object to what he was doing. As the ships sailed closer to Cuba the world waited. If the United States sank the Soviet ships, war was almost inevitable.

Khrushchev was really trying to see just how far the American president was prepared to go, and finally ordered the ships to turn around. The Soviets then agreed to remove the missiles already installed on Cuba, in return for a promise from the United States not to invade the island. The crisis was over and war had been avoided, but it had been close. To try to prevent future misunderstandings, a direct **hot-line** telephone link was set up between the US capital Washington and the Soviet capital Moscow.

Map legend:
- III Soviet missile bases
- ----- US naval blockade

CANADA

USA

SEATTLE
SAN FRANCISCO
LAS VEGAS
LOS ANGELES
DENVER
KANSAS CITY
NASHVILLE
OKLAHOMA CITY
DALLAS
CHICAGO
NEW YORK
BOSTON
WASHINGTON
NEW ORLEANS
MIAMI

2500km range from Cuba
2000km range from Cuba
1000km range from Cuba

GULF OF MEXICO
MEXICO
ATLANTIC OCEAN
HAVANA
CUBA

N

0 km   1000 km
0 miles   620 miles

Soviet nuclear missiles had a range of over 2,500 kilometres (1,550 miles). If fired from Cuba, almost all of the United States was in danger.

Discrediting Castro

In 1962 US military chiefs began thinking of ways that they could discredit or harm Fidel Castro. Among the suggestions were:

- Sink a boat load of refugees crossing from Cuba to the United States and blame Castro.

- Be prepared to blame Castro if the 1962 space flight carrying John Glenn crashed.

- Prepare a poisoned scuba-diving suit as a gift for Castro.

- Blow up an American warship and blame it on Castro.

Fortunately none of these ideas was carried out.

Hungary and Czechoslovakia

Although the Soviet Union controlled the communist governments of Eastern Europe very strictly, there were still times when Soviet military strength was needed to keep some of them in line. Two such examples were Hungary and Czechoslovakia.

The Hungarian rebellion

When Stalin died in 1953, Khrushchev – his successor – criticized him for not having given the people of Eastern Europe more freedom. The Hungarian people hoped that this meant they could have **freedom of speech** and the right to follow their Catholic Christian religion.

In 1956 the Hungarian Prime Minister, Imre Nagy, announced that Hungary would leave the Warsaw Pact. This Pact was an alliance of all the communist countries in Eastern Europe. It had been set up in 1955 to oppose the North Atlantic Treaty Organization (NATO), a military organization formed by the Western powers in 1949.

Khrushchev feared that if Hungary left the Warsaw Pact, other communist countries might do the same, so on 4 November 1956 he sent 200,000 troops into Hungary. Many Hungarians took up arms to defend their country, but Hungary was soon back under Soviet control. Over 27,000 Hungarians died in the rebellion. Nagy was taken to Moscow and hanged.

Soviet tanks patrol the streets of Budapest, the capital of Hungary, in November 1956 during the crushing of the Hungarian rebellion.

A drawing on a wall of a Prague street in 1968. It shows how in 1945 the Soviet army had been welcomed because it freed Czechoslovakia from German rule. But in 1968 the army returned as attackers.

The Prague Spring

In 1968 the Czechoslovak leader, Alexander Dubček, began to make changes in Czechoslovakia to give people more freedom. He permitted foreign travel, ended **censorship**, and allowed public meetings and discussions. People described his changes as the "Prague Spring" because there was a thaw from the old harsh way of life. Dubček reassured the Soviet leader Leonid Brezhnev (who had taken over from Khrushchev in 1964) that Czechoslovakia had no intention of leaving the Warsaw Pact and that the changes were no threat to the Soviet Union.

Brezhnev was not convinced. On 21 August 1968 Soviet troops invaded Czechoslovakia. The Soviet soldiers had been told that they were there at the invitation of the Czechoslavak government to put down troublemakers. They could not understand why the Czechoslavak people jeered and spat at them. Dubček was arrested and dismissed. Soviet authority was restored, and the changes Dubček had made were reversed.

A plea from a Hungarian radio station

"Civilized people of the world, listen and come to our aid with soldiers and arms. Do not forget that there is no stopping the wild attack of communism. Your turn will come, once we perish."

When this broadcast was made in November 1956, Soviet troops were advancing into Hungary. Despite the pleas for help, the West did nothing to stop the Russian invasion.

The Vietnam war

The Soviet Union had stood back from provoking war over the Cuban missile crisis, but in the 1960s the Americans and Soviets came close to direct fighting over Vietnam, in Asia.

A divided country

Vietnam was divided into two countries. North Vietnam was a communist country, receiving money and support from the Soviet Union. South Vietnam was an anti-communist country; however, its government was having trouble with communist **guerillas** in its territory. The guerillas, known as the Vietcong, were receiving support from North Vietnam and the Soviet Union. They wanted to overthrow the South Vietnamese government and set up a communist government in its place.

The Americans were concerned that if South Vietnam became communist then, one by one, the countries surrounding it would fall – like dominoes knocking each other over. They called this the "Domino Theory".

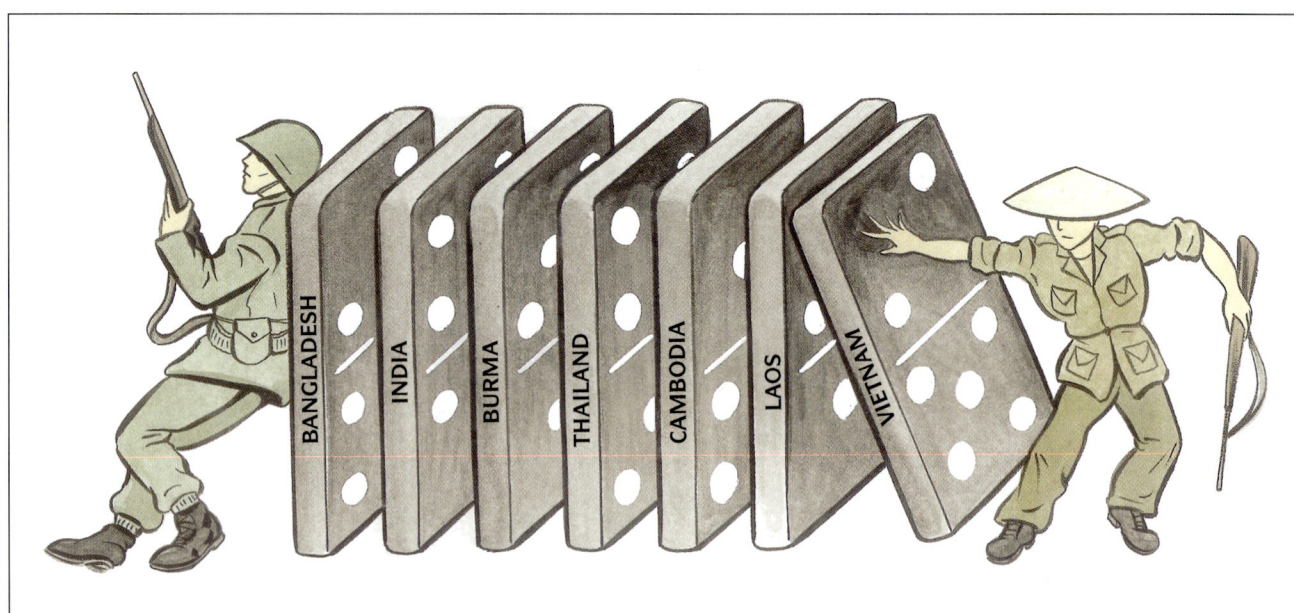

The Domino Theory – if one country falls to communism, it takes the rest with it.

American troops in action in the Vietnam war

War begins and ends

Between 1954 and 1960 the Americans sent experts to help train the South Vietnamese army to fight against the Vietcong. The United States said these people were advisors, but really they were military officers and soldiers. Despite US help, the South Vietnamese could not defeat the Vietcong, so the United States sent more troops. By 1965 there were over 180,000 US troops in Vietnam, but they found it very difficult to defeat an army skilled in jungle warfare. By 1968 the majority of Americans were not prepared to tolerate the cost of the war or the terrible attacks on innocent villagers that were sometimes carried out by frustrated US soldiers.

In 1973 US President Richard Nixon negotiated a ceasefire and American troops left Vietnam. The war had cost 58,000 US lives and a million Vietnamese. By 1976 North Vietnam had over-run South Vietnam and joined the two countries together as one communist country.

A nuclear deterrent?

It is interesting to note that although the US military had numerous nuclear weapons, it did not use them in Vietnam – even though they could not win the war. Despite having huge numbers of weapons, the United States and the Soviet Union were careful not to use them. The main purpose of having nuclear weapons was to make enemy countries too frightened to attack. This is called the nuclear deterrent.

Unfreezing the Cold War

The arms race

During the Cold War both sides raced to create a supply of weapons superior to that of their opponent. This became known as the "arms race". The build-up not only threatened world peace, but it was also extremely expensive. A lot of schools and hospitals can be built for the price of a nuclear submarine!

The British athlete Alan Wells won the 100 metre gold medal at the 1980 Moscow Olympics. Some experts argue that he was able to win this medal only because the United States did not send a team to Moscow, following the Soviet Union's invasion of Afghanistan.

It is not surprising, therefore, that during the Cold War there were occasions when the leaders of the Soviet Union and the United States tried to reach agreements to limit spending on arms and reduce tension between the two sides. Such was the level of distrust between them, however, that this proved very difficult.

Détente

During the Cuban missile crisis, President Kennedy suggested to the Soviet Union that they should aim to have détente, a lessening of the tension between the two sides. The setting up of the hot-line after the Cuban missile crisis was the first step towards this. However, from 1965, relations between the United States and the Soviet Union actually got worse as they argued over Vietnam and Czechoslovakia.

Breakthrough

A major breakthrough came in 1972 when the two sides signed an agreement at the end of the Strategic Arms Limitation Talks (SALT). It said that they would limit the number of nuclear missiles they were producing. In 1975 the United States and Soviet Union both signed the Helsinki Accord on **human rights** and in 1979 there was another agreement about limiting arms (SALT 2). Then on Christmas Day 1979 the Soviet Union invaded Afghanistan. Good relations between the United States and the Soviet Union broke down, SALT 2 was abandoned, and the United States refused to attend the 1980 Olympic Games in Moscow.

Reagan and Gorbachev

It took a change of presidency in both countries to bring about a genuine improvement in relations. In 1981 Ronald Reagan became US president and in 1985 Mikhail Gorbachev became the Soviet leader. Gorbachev knew that the Soviet Union was bankrupt and he wanted to reduce spending on defence. Reagan was very suspicious of the Soviets, but many of his advisors wanted a more peaceful relationship with the Soviet Union. Reagan was also keen to cut taxation in the United States and saw arms reduction as a way of doing this.

In November 1985 the two leaders met in Geneva, Switzerland, and immediately established good relations. They soon agreed to reduce nuclear missiles in Europe and began discussions on reducing non-nuclear weapons too. However, before any agreement could be reached on non-nuclear weapons, astonishing changes occurred in Europe.

Reagan and Gorbachev met in Geneva in November 1985.

The end of the Cold War

Glasnost and Perestroika

Although Mikhail Gorbachev was very successful in bringing about improved relations with the West, he was less successful at home. He followed two main policies. *Perestroika* was the reshaping of the Soviet economy to allow more profit-making by individuals and to reduce control by the government. *Glasnost* meant more openness about government and more freedom of speech. Criticism of government policy was allowed and attempts were made to cut corruption among government officials.

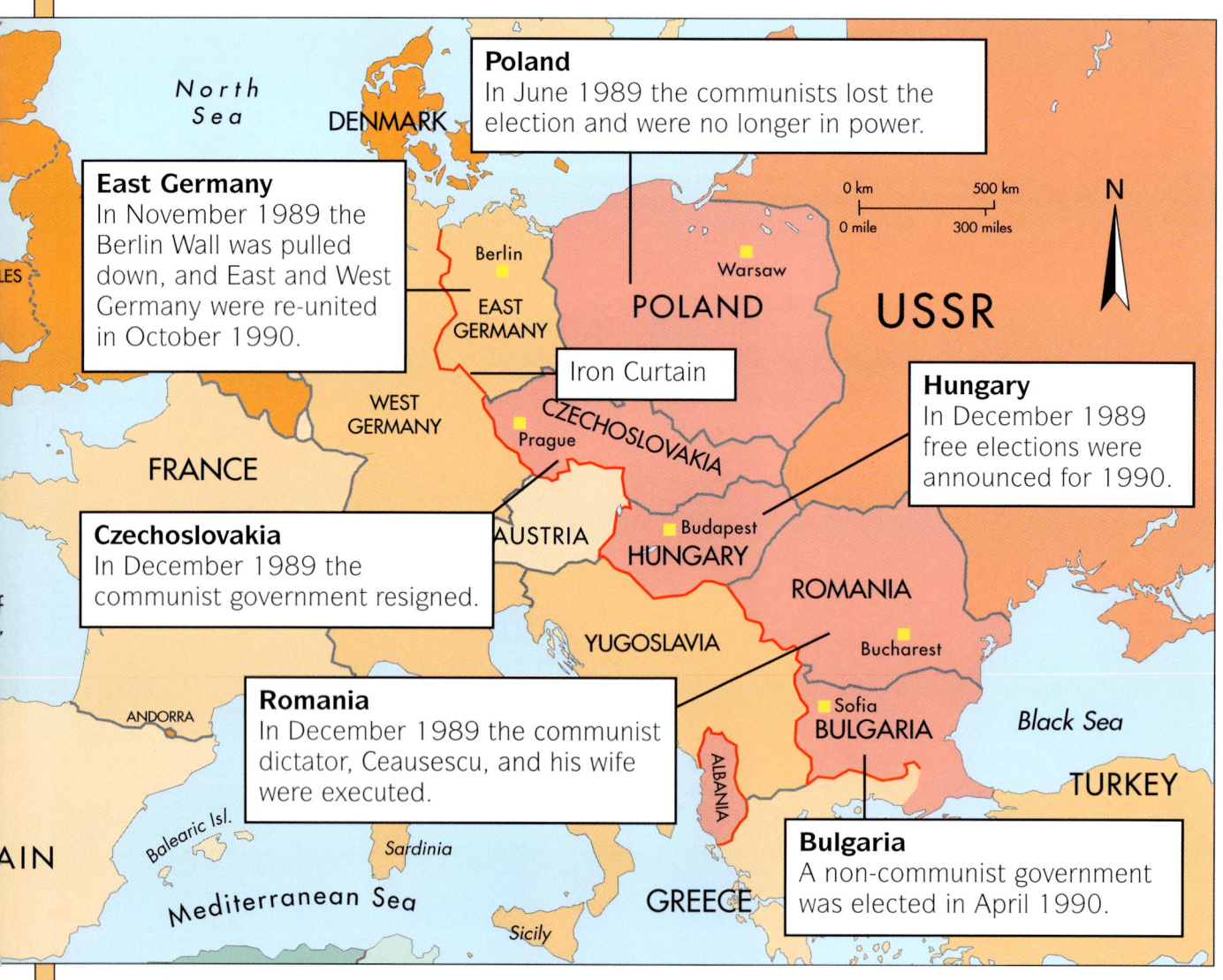

Poland
In June 1989 the communists lost the election and were no longer in power.

East Germany
In November 1989 the Berlin Wall was pulled down, and East and West Germany were re-united in October 1990.

Iron Curtain

Hungary
In December 1989 free elections were announced for 1990.

Czechoslovakia
In December 1989 the communist government resigned.

Romania
In December 1989 the communist dictator, Ceausescu, and his wife were executed.

Bulgaria
A non-communist government was elected in April 1990.

The events of 1989–90 that led to the end of communism in Europe

While horrifying traditional Soviet communists, at the same time Gorbachev's policies led the people of the Soviet Union to expect greater changes than could be managed. Soon the country was in turmoil as people from all sides criticized the Soviet leader and his government.

The fall of the Soviet empire

The weakening of the control of the government was soon noticed by opponents of communism in Europe. The days when opposition to communism would mean Soviet tanks being sent in to deal with "troublemakers" were long past. Suddenly the people of Eastern Europe realized that they no longer had anything to fear from the Soviet Union. Between May 1989 and March 1990 communist governments were overthrown in Hungary, East Germany, Bulgaria, Romania, and Czechoslovakia. The Iron Curtain had dissolved. In November 1989 the Berlin Wall was pulled down, and just one year later East and West Germany were re-united.

In December 1989 Gorbachev and George Bush, Senior, the new American president, announced that the Cold War was over. Gorbachev was awarded the **Nobel Peace Prize** in 1990.

The end of the wall

"What was my reaction the other night? I tell you. I'm a hard old retired colonel, but I had tears in my eyes. To see people standing on the wall, where once they would have been shot. I could hardly take it all in."

These comments were made by American pilot Gail S. Halvorsen after the fall of the Berlin Wall. Halvorsen was called the "Berlin candy bomber" because of his work during the Berlin airlift.

The great debate

The West believes the collapse of Soviet communism benefited everyone, but democracy does not flourish everywhere and not everyone is better off.

Question 1: Has the collapse of communism brought greater freedom?

Yes!

- The people of countries such as Poland, Hungary, and the Czech Republic have many new freedoms.
- They can elect their government, hold public meetings, belong to trade unions, and worship freely.
- Everyone must obey the law and there is freedom of speech.
- Several Eastern European states, such as the Czech Republic and Poland, have been welcomed into the democratic European Union.

No!

- Several ex-communist states are not really democracies.
- The governments of Turkmenistan and Uzbekistan are perhaps even more tyrannical than in Soviet times.
- Several other states, such as Kyrgyzstan, Tajikistan, and Azerbaijan, are not successful democracies.
- Some argue that the Russians themselves do not enjoy democratic freedom.
- Areas such as Georgia, Azerbaijan, and Chechnya have been torn apart by bloody civil wars since 1990.
- After the collapse of communism, Russian troops remained in several ex-Soviet states, such as Georgia and Tajikistan.

Have the good effects of the fall of the Berlin Wall and European communism been exaggerated?

What do you think?

A map of the present-day Commonwealth of Independent States. Do these countries really enjoy greater freedoms now?

Question 2: Are people better off since the fall of communism?

Yes!

- Capitalism allows hard-working, successful, and fortunate individuals – like the Russian billionaire Roman Abramovitch – to make their fortunes.

- Capitalism encourages competition, which improves quality and choice.

- Capitalist countries are richer than communist ones, so there is more money to share around.

No!

- Communism guaranteed everyone food, a job, medical care, a pension, and a home. Although these were not always of good quality, under capitalism poverty, ill-health, and even starvation are often possible.

- In Russia and most other ex-communist states crime has soared since 1990.

- Public services, such as bus and rail transport, often worked better under communism.

- Communists have faith in human nature, believing we can create a perfect world; capitalists believe we do things primarily for ourselves.

Is the world really better off since the fall of the Berlin Wall?

What do you think?

Find out more

Using the Internet

Explore the Internet to find out more about the fall of the Berlin Wall. You can use a search engine, such as www.yahooligans.com or www.google.com, and type in keywords or phrases such as *communism*, *capitalism*, *Vietnam war*, *Cold war*, or *Castro*.

More books to read

Ross, Stewart. Witness to History: The Collapse of Communism. (Heinemann Library, 2004)

Sheehan, Sean. Questioning History: The Cold War. (Hodder Children's Books, 2003)

Tames, Richard and Downing, David. Political and Economic Systems: Capitalism. (Heinemann Library, 2003)

Tames, Richard and Downing, David. Political and Economic Systems: Communism. (Heinemann Library, 2003)

Timeline

1917	November	Communist revolution in Russia
1939	August	Nazi–Soviet Pact signed
1941	June	Hitler invades Soviet Union
1946	March	Churchill makes his Iron Curtain speech
1947	March	Truman makes his Truman Doctrine speech
	June	Marshall Plan announced
1948	June	Berlin blockade; start of airlift
1949		Formation of NATO
1953		Death of Stalin
1955		Formation of Warsaw Pact
1956	November	Soviet tanks enter Hungary
1961	June	Kennedy makes "Ich bin ein Berliner" speech
	August	Construction of Berlin Wall begins
1962	October	Cuban missile crisis
1968		Beginning of Prague Spring
1972	May	SALT Agreement signed
1973	January	Ceasefire agreed in Vietnam
1975		Helsinki Accord signed
1976		Communist troops over-run South Vietnam
1979	December	Soviet Union invades Afghanistan
1980	July	Moscow Olympics boycotted by United States
1985	March	Gorbachev becomes Soviet leader
1989	May	Break up of Warsaw Pact begins
	November	Fall of Berlin Wall
	December	Bush and Gorbachev announce end of Cold War
1990		Germany re-united
		Gorbachev receives Nobel Peace Prize
1991	August	Attempted coup against Gorbachev. Communist Party disbanded.
	December	Soviet Union disbanded
2001		European Court of Human Rights sends three East German communist leaders to jail for having allowed shooting of fugitives at Berlin Wall

Glossary

allies	countries that agree to help each other, especially in time of war
appeasement	policy of trying to avoid war by negotiation
Berlin Wall	fortified border built to divide East and West Berlin
blockade	preventing supplies reaching a city or island
Bolshevik	name of the political group later known as the Communist Party
capitalism/ capitalists	person or system that allows private ownership of land and industry, and where the owners keep the profits
censorship	when newspapers and other media are forbidden to print or say some things
civil war	war between people in the same country
Cold War	when countries are political enemies, but are not actually fighting each other in a full-scale war
communism	classless society in which personal freedom and enterprise are limited
communist	person or state that follows communism
democracy	system of government where leaders are elected by the people
freedom of speech	right to express a view without fear of punishment
guerillas	fighters who carry out ambushes and small-scale attacks
hot-line	telephone link between important heads of state
human right	something that people ought to be able to have or do freely
Iron Curtain	an expression describing how the democratic countries of Europe were separated from the communist ones after World War II
labour camps	prison camp where people are forced to do long hours of hard physical work for no pay
Marshall Plan	plan to give American economic aid to countries resisting communism
Nazi	name used to describe Hitler's political party and brutal style of government
Nobel Peace Prize	prize awarded for making outstanding contributions to the welfare of humankind
propaganda	twisting of information to portray a particular point of view
Soviet Union	name of union of states in former Russia after the revolution of 1917. Also called the Union of Soviet Socialist Republics (USSR).
superpowers	name given to the United States and the Soviet Union after World War II
Truman Doctrine	US policy of helping countries resist communism
tsar	name of the Russian head of state before the revolution of 1917

Index